Kintsugi: Poems of Hope & Healing

Maryam Daftari

1st WORLD
PUBLISHING

Kintsugi: Poems of Hope & Healing
Maryam Daftari

Copyright © 2023 Maryam Daftari

Published by 1st World Publishing
P.O. Box 2211, Fairfield, Iowa 52556
tel: 641-209-5000 • fax: 866-440-5234
web: www.1stworldpublishing.com

First Edition
Library of Congress cataloging-in-Publication Data
ISBN: 978-1-4218-3550-1

Contents

"...what I want in my life
is to be willing
to be dazzled —
to cast aside the weight of facts

and maybe even
to float a little
above this difficult world.
I want to believe I am looking

into the white fire of a great mystery.
I want to believe that the imperfections are nothing —
that the light is everything — that it is more than the sum
of each flawed blossom rising and fading. And I do."

— Mary Oliver, "The Ponds" from *House of Light*

Dedication

To my beloved son and best friend, Ali

Introduction

Over the course of the last three plus years – a period that would inevitably become etched in our collective memories – isolation emerged as an unwelcome companion: one we were forced to coexist with, often against our will. This book reflects the resonances of those long stretches of solitude, the silent, or at times, eerie echoes that pervaded most of our homes and hearts.

There was a monumental struggle, almost a battle between life and death that we, as a species found ourselves entangled in. Emerging from this tumultuous period, we began to treasure what we had always had, but perhaps took for granted — connections, the warmth of human contact, the privilege of being in the comforting presence of our loved ones without the specter of a pandemic. It was akin to the birth of a new realization: love, in its myriad wonders, became the precious gold, filling the cracks, the loneliness in our lives. It served as the potent healing element in our 'kintsugi,' the Japanese art of mending broken pottery with gold or silver, metaphorically transforming our life into a vessel made more beautiful by its finely repaired fractures, creating an even more unique and stronger piece of art through the principle of embracing imperfections and flaws.

Within the pages of this poetry book lies a journey of introspection, where the beauty of imperfections is accepted, even celebrated through the connection that perhaps can best be described using two Japanese philosophies of *kintsugi* and *wabi-sabi* that invite us to pause, reflect, and find solace in the imperfect, transient nature of existence, takes the notion of imperfections to another level by infusing it with the spirit of resilience and renewal: an art of repairing broken pottery with lacquer mixed with powdered gold, silver, or platinum.

Rather than hiding the cracks, kintsugi celebrates them, turning them into intricate veins of gold, transforming what was once broken into something even more unique and attractive, emphasizing that scars or repairs are not something to be concealed or discarded but rather a testament to the strength and character of any object or person.

Wabi-sabi, a concept deeply rooted in Japanese aesthetics, reminds us of the *inherent beauty found in simplicity*, impermanence, and the natural world – to embrace the imperfect and the weathered, urging us to appreciate fleeting moments, to find beauty and contentment in the unadorned and unpretentious.

In this collection of poems, we thus delve into the philosophy of kintsugi, and by extension, into wabi-sabi, allowing that profound wisdom to seep into our thoughts and actions.

Through the exploration of nature, and life's ups and downs, we come to accept, even embrace this fleeting nature of life and the necessity of finding power within our own weaknesses. Each poem shines light into the cracks or fractures of our lives, and the 'gold' that has perhaps mended them, a tolerance for imperfections that have shaped us, and an invitation to find solace in our shared experiences and vulnerabilities.

Social distancing brought about seclusion, and a forced isolation. It initially meant relative safety and decreasing risk, but rapidly transformed into loneliness which brought about its own slew of issues and challenges.

Some tried to make the best of this awkward and for some, debilitating isolation, attempting introspection, an opportunity for deep pondering and reflection. But despite its veneer of peace and opportunity it granted some to turn inwards, it lacked much that we needed, for it had an absence at its core — that although meditations and the beauty of nature did help — they could not completely replace that yearning for the nourishment of love.

Thus did the "kintsugi path" to our healing process reside in the tenets of connection, empathy, compassion, and caring, all enveloped in this single potent word, "love." It is love's unparalleled ability to incite our deepest yearnings, our constant quest for joy, happiness, and inner bliss.

As we delve into this collection of verse, we explore and celebrate the "kintsugi of love" in all its forms and nuances, gifting us with healing. I hope these verses serve as a gentle reminder that perhaps perfection is an illusion, and beauty may encompass the appreciation of life's imperfections. May they inspire us to discover the extraordinary within the ordinary, finding joy in the intricate dynamics of hope between brokenness and healing.

***

The first section of the book, "Pandemic Days," explores the various emotions and experiences that come with living through a pandemic: from the gripping fears and disbeliefs, to moments of hope, light and inspiration that shine through, helping us navigate the uncertainties. We are reminded of the strength and resilience of the human spirit, the power of hope and determination in the face of sometimes insurmountable fear, doubt, and loneliness, with an underlying message of self-compassion and growth in the face of adversity.

Poems in this section delve into the complexities of living in a world plagued for two plus years by crescendos in illness, stress, or loss but also hope. Through poems like "We are the Torchbearers," "Hope," and "Healing Trickling," I aim to provide glimmers of light in the seemingly gathering clouds, that we are stronger together, helping one another even if we have been temporarily separated — to take the art of kintsugi to the societal level of communities through inclusiveness and caring — like mending broken chinaware with powdered gold, by reestablishing neglected social bonds and the blessings of face to face encounters.

***

The second section, "The Dao of the Warrior" is an invitation to reflect on the wisdom and ways of ancient warriors, contemporary ones in the midst of battles to survive, to embrace our inner warrior as we face challenges in order to seek to overcome obstacles.

This section references Russia's invasion of Ukraine, its traumatic consequences, and an analysis of war through the unique ancient Chinese treatise: Sun Tzu's "The Art of War," which lauds the importance of "moral influence" or "right path" of leaders engaged in the conduct of war. If we were to apply the principles and strategies that Sun Tzu outlines in his military treatise, we could see that he would have probably predicted that since Ukraine has the moral high ground, whatever the outcome of the battles, Ukraine would ultimately emerge victorious.

I pay homage to the great spiritual and actual warriors; some old, some new: tapping into their teachings as a source of inspirational guidance. From "Sun Tzu" to "Unveiling the Scarf Rebellion," topics explore themes of bravery and determination in the face of battles, the inner and outer.

Together we celebrate the wonders of the human spirit, and the many ways in which it allows us to rise to the challenges of life and access the light within. If you are a lover of poetry, or simply seeking inspiration and comfort, I hope these poems, written during different periods of the pandemic, will be a source of solace and insight, as we strive to live our best lives.

Foreword

In Mary Oliver's poem, "Breakage," a speaker at the edge of the sea encounters "nothing at all whole" but rather fragments "tattered" and "split," shining in the morning light. This "schoolhouse/of little words" speaks first of individual meanings that hint at a "whole story."

Maryam Daftari, too, finds herself on borders and edges, emerging into our post-pandemic moment that feels anything but whole. With bravery, wit, and insight, she gamely accepts the challenge put forth by lyricists like Oliver and Robert Frost who wonder what we might "make of a diminished thing."

This is the substance, work, and passion at the core of Daftari's moving collection of poems. This isn't merely the work of a poet keen in the arts of observation and description. Her work embraces the fractures and fragments from the world and gathers them into lyrics that somehow make our time, spaces, and selves feel whole again. Daftari has found inspiration from the Japanese art of Kintsugi, in which veins of gold and silver repair what's broken, beauty scars that eschew concealment and celebrate a simultaneity of breakage, healing, and transformation.

Early in the collection she asks, "What is the story we are left to tell?" In poems that range from meditative reflections to the more spirited persuasions of a social justice warrior, Daftari, even amidst contemporary moments of contagion and conflict, reminds us that any day is "a day that could change everything,/…A day to make …our mark." Here is a voice that invites you to walk with her, to embrace the necessary work of the heart and mind and move towards connection and healing. In privileging the process of unification and repair, her lyrics – complexes of blemish and beauty – gift us a "new opening/to fill the empty cup" and yield a sea-change of resilience and affirmation.

Michael Morse
Author of *Void and Compensation*

Section 1 - Pandemic Days

During the pandemic, we were all on a warrior path, experiencing a wide range of emotions and challenges, fears and uncertainties of potentially life-threatening situations, causing great stress and anxiety. Many were forced to separate from loved ones in order to protect them from the virus — a difficult, emotionally painful time.

Some experienced loss of family members and friends in traumatic, heart-wrenching circumstances. In addition, the economic and societal effects of the pandemic were severe, with so many losing jobs, struggling to make ends meet, and feeling isolated.

Despite hardships and sacrifices people faced, there were moments of hope, faith and resilience. Many people came together to support one another and help those in need. Some found solace walking outdoors, appreciating the beauty in nature.

Although the pandemic was a long and distressing stretch in our lives, it also brought out the best in people, as they demonstrated love, compassion, resilience, and strength in the face of adversity. On this "warrior path," it was all about hoping and healing!

Be Gentle with Yourself

Be gentle with yourself,
precious one,
the earth has
only one like you —
so be tender
with yourself.

Keep the smile
that lights the path
to friends to make amends,
be gentle as you go.
This journey may be long or short —
so be thoughtful as you go.

Innocence learns on the road
like bringing the spare tire
of hope-courage combined,
the windings and the climbs
a free-for-all on this
frozen mountain pass

with hidden twists and turns —
so be gentle as you go.
With no end in sight,
just the play of light and night
be gentle with yourself today,
aware of all the fray

to leave it all behind
on the other side of the day.

We are the Torchbearers

Carrying the light within
to light the melancholy
of our missing ones
All those who have given up
keeping their inner light burning.

The pandemic extinguished so many candles,
left burning down to the wick.
Church candles continue to glow,
the moon still visits nightly, distant yet here.
The sun always rises to show eternal light .

What is the story we are left to tell?
This story that must be told –
to keep the light within burning.
A story of hope – for we are
the torchbearers of it.

IN JAPAN, BROKEN OBJECTS are OFTEN REPAIRED WITH GOLD. THE FLAW is SEEN as A UNIQUE PIECE OF the OBJECT'S HISTORY, WHICH ADDS TO its BEAUTY.

CONSIDER THIS
WHEN YOU FEEL BROKEN.

Walk with Me

Noting the unwellness and brokenness within,
Filling cracks with the gold of smiles and hopes,
Smoothing rough edges with silver linings,
Kintsugi walks with me

Like a skilled seamstress at her loom.
Kintsugi's art — no superficial feat,
Healing deep the wounds and broken pieces,
Fitting life's puzzle with platinum to complete,

Finds and repairs what eludes and ceases.
Is it the magic of soothing comfort,
Like a mother's kind touch and healing,
A salve for wounds and scars of time?

A balm for hurts that leave us reeling?
Kintsugi's healing — felt and witnessed,
Like magic in the lighted shiny cracks,
The power for renewal and pure consciousness,

As ambrosia seeps and settles in the cracks.
And so I hug kintsugi my friend,
Grateful for its 'gold powder' and healing art,
A reminder — that brokenness can be mended,
And connectedness shine again in every heart.

How to Travel in a Pandemic

In my mind's whispers, like a sutra, I move freely.
Today, to the comfort of a secluded Daoist monastery
I visited many times in bustling Hong Kong,
where devotees bowed and lighted joss sticks,
prayed before ancestor ashes niched inside,
with photos of the deceased on display like library books.

Another whisper in stillness returns me to the lake in
Fairfield at Waterworks Park in Iowa, woods around it
still resonant with afternoon strolls with friends.
This whispered gift lay there, waiting, untouched inside
me, until a pandemic unearths these secrets of the mind.
I journey, feel tranquility here, anytime my mind whispers.

The mind whispers again: "Back to the ocean!" I follow
like a loyal swallow returning home, now to the
Yogananda Gardens overlooking an eternal blue.
I sit once again on a stone bench warmed by the sun,
eyes focus, ears connect to the mantra of the waves.
Movement & rest, everlasting duality, in mind & reality

Here I stay. I dip in bliss –
for how long I do not know — until
whispers awaken again and I travel
in my mind — without —
the hassles of travel in a pandemic.

Heart Torn

Weary of the slow-motion pace of days
behaves mostly in silence, this bosom companion,
dragging us to places we refuse to travel, with some
lingering, as though conniving with the invisible,

unholy Covid spikes – there, over there,
those outlines, mirage-like, witches stoop over pots
stirring evil potions meant to harm.
Yes, hard times are upon us

but then — they cannot go on forever.
No storm lasts forever, says the Daoist,
but hope outlasts the storm.
Yet your pain, my pain, is our pain —

permeating mind and body, and maybe,
the storm cannot win, maybe we shall.
Haven't we been told that hard times strength us,
like fire making steel? Like the flexible bamboo

that bends with the wind and adapts — not breaking?
The past never stops speaking, and the future,
we cannot hope to hear — its very nature secretive,
yet revealing to a few wisest of sages and believers.

So 'tis the present that can analyze aptly,
having learned from the past, the bitter and sweet,
takes the reins of history's horses and chariot —
like a seer who knows the path.

I Am No Sculptor

But I can carve this handy Tuesday I have, although
it was unforgiving last week, and I shall tell you why its
jagged profile — challenging to take on
not a place or time to be careless.

This Tuesday — mine to sculpt — the mother of all
    Tuesdays:

I could be on Snake Island with all its wreckage —
graveyard of military hardware but I am here —
this fragile Tuesday — not over there in sub-freezing
temperatures on a dirigible boat stuck on a sandbar in
    darkness.

Not in the middle of a war — on Snake Island, now,

in Ukrainian hands under Russian missiles, not a place to
    be careless about.
But then — I remember Snake Alley in Burlington, Iowa
    — maybe
the crookedest alley in the world, overlooking the library
    where we
delighted in workshopping poetry with the Society of
    Great River Poets.

Or, I could be in war weary Afghanistan

after America finally abandoned the endless war, as
others had like the Soviets before, where today,
Tuesday, Taliban announced women would be banned
   from
studying at universities — what's left of them.

I could be in Kurdish Sanandaj

protesting the hejab and being arrested —
with a maghnaeh forced on my head —
and many other bewildered innocent heads —
which could be the next to be hanged.

But I'm here this precious Tuesday in Carlsbad

where a gunman might shoot someone while I shop at
Walmart for some flatbread and goat cheese for lunch.
I'm here where fires rampage and
droughts can scrape on — for years.

Yes, I could be back again in vibrant Hong Kong,

walking down Central in the crowd before the PRC
ran over freedom, where I looked for jade in the sea of
   jewelry
displays or dined at City Hall with its never- ending

27

carts of piled-high dim sum treats on Tuesdays.

Yes, but I am here — still here on this Tuesday —

cautious of all the viruses queuing for hosts alongside
the partisan bickering that goes on ad nauseam.
Yes, it's very punctual this Tuesday.
I know not where fate will call us to serve,

I'll embrace this Tuesday, this moment

in time – where hope replaces despair
to see where the journey leads –
one day at a time – for we
are the sculptors of each day that dawns.

This Tuesday, a day like any other,

But also a day that could change everything,
A day to seize and hold onto,
A day to make a difference,
to make our mark.

Between Despair and Hope

In this whirlwind of our lives, I'm not in any
celebratory mood. Of course, I am thankful —
still walking this earth, yet hard to smile, to laugh —
when so many in fear or illness remain.

When much is at stake, & like mountain scaling, so
daunting to ascend. This pandemic, darkening our lives,
we try to save what remnants of hope linger — chorus of
prayers in our heads for healing, for true harmony.

***

The storm feels as if it could last forever — no end to
these struggles, the pinnacle covered in a fog of despair,
tears feed our rivers, with all the political squabbles &
stalemate, making the water more stagnant.

This makes what we already miss in our 'new normal' lives
hollower, & the disconcerting mutiplicty in the market of
alternative facts, adds to already wounded truths that
hurt our social conscience even more.

This residue of stress, uncertainties, taste like stale bread, a lingering taste, maybe familiar from our lonely-filled moments.

How must we await the light? Like dawn? Words of Emerson circle back: "Life is an apprenticeship to the truth, that around every circle another can be drawn…in every end there is a beginning."

After an end to the unsettling period of 'normalization' of untruths & distortion of realities, a new beginning, a new dawn will descend, & we squint, hoping, that the cloudy greys of countless dawns will give rise

to the sun's glorious countenance, to light up not only our faces, but our inner light of strengths, & once again — we overcome. And the rusty chimes shall find their voices — & ring once again.

Filling the Cracks

Examining, then filling the unwellness & broken in us
with smiles & hopes of gold fillings
to smooth over rough edges with some of its silver
linings too, like a skilled seamstress repairing
ancient tapestry with gold threads & expertise.

Kintsugi — no superficial artist, heals deep down the hurt
pieces, fitting the mended parts in the broken puzzle
of life's pains: the platinum fills what's missing.
Kintsugi's magic — knows what & where to repair
this brokenness that may elude us.

Is it the magic of its soothing comfort — like a mother's
loving embrace? A kindness that heals the wounds of
time? The healing there to witness — kintsugi's gold
powder to mend the damaged pot or bowl, like a mantra
to help unite the dive — to an awareness of unity

in connectedness, the ambrosia that heals, like light
seeping through the cracks — the power for healing.

Talbots

I once loved to walk the endless aisles of clothing
in all colors, even those that hurt my eyes.
What was the fashion that long-ago year? The stylish hues?

A few days ago, for the first time since the pandemic hit,
I dared enter a shop, masked, — a foreboding sense of
  'Delta Dread'
took over — as though I were not just entering Talbots,
  but Talbots' den.

Nothing seemed to bite me. Few customers were
around,

still I kept my distance.
I looked around at colors I once liked.
They left me grey and cold.
I wonderd why.

Gone the desire or attachment to own new clothes
In fact, I liked being someone with no new clothes,
a rejection — of the pre-pandemic past.
There was no going back.

***

A friend of mine from New York plays her own game —
dresses up everyday with one of her fancy pre-pandemic
  outfits
along with her prized jewelry. She puts each photo on
  Facebook
to brighten not only her own day, but all those who
  "LIKE" her.

A strange kind of masquerade party of one!

Up

I visualize a steady climb ahead
up the narrow wobbly ladder of life.
It takes me up, yes, up —
creaky warning sounds,
my shaky hands,
faltering feet,

swaying between hope & despair.
I focus on each rail of hope,
feel the brevity of each.
My heart — unsteady too,
I dare not look down
or up or sideways.

Gazing straight ahead towards a perceived balance.
Mind ascends with body,
& I repeat: "Stay centered, calm & climb on."
Fear may contradict itself, vacillates here & there
on this steady unsteady climb. I feel each rung
as one feels every stone crossing a river,

a sign of triumph or a fall.

Scars to Strengths

Acts of compassion, tenderness. and reconnecting
pour in — the glued gold powder that binds the shards.
Light trickles in, to shine through the cracks —
recovering a facet thought lost. Hurt lives — in parts of the
    past — in this, our history too.

Difficult as the pandemic was, yet challenges remained
— some turned into golden opportunities for healing
    again.
Kintsugi reminds that scars are not imperfections,
just healable battle scars, sources of strength on journeys
of self-discovery & transformations to heal.

Stories of resilience — steadfastness & courage to share:
remembering those less fortunate, like mountain climbers,
holding weaker hands while scaling treacherous terrain, to
find more power from the ascent together, a renewal, the
    light of wellness like sunrise again.

How to escape this epidemic of isolation & loneliness?
Society's brokenness? Communities like broken pots, need
repair through social reconnections, our "polarities" need

time & wisdom to link up again. This, the 'kintsugi road-map,' from a kind of social recession to recovery's healing.

Establishing once again abandoned, if not fractured relationships — retrieving neglected bonds — akin to mending "broken vessels"— to emerge out of the shadows, restoring vibrancy to lives through blessings of face to face encounters whether in packed coffee shops, sports or musical events — all await us.

Joy of Seasons

Once again, stepping into life's "new normal,"
after a never-ending chain of monastic days
where warriors of peace sacrificed in endless pains.
A hopeful post-crisis stroll for some,
and by & by,

to hear again Nature's songs in semi-secret hums
to feel again the gentle strums
of lively summers moving on — yet time will tell,
what Nature holds close to breast,
but by & by

as Iowa's cornstalks begin to age today,
& California pomegranates blush over here,
with various trees reluctant to be bare again,
yet by & by, still — times of slow recovery,

inequalities in work & pay depress
slow motion times of burning discontent may
turn to vanishing warmth & fall's steady footsteps
echoing forth, by & by,

as pumpkins fatten, & bird songs fade,
autumn's tones parade in flying harmony
with trees clad in fiery leaves, predicting
by & by,

that battles with nuclear threats will rage away
while prayerful hopes whisper wild & high,
for peace & less solitude —
just bonding days for all to join again.

Healing Trickling

When acts of compassion & kindness flow
Like molten gold — binds shattered pieces whole,
Where hope & light peek, shining through the cracks,
Renewal's born despite life's rolling toll

Hurt lives, echoes of past & recent traumas of history,
Challenges of pandemic faced with forebearance,
Flipped into golden opportunities to spare what's left
With more caring & reconnecting queuing.

Kintsugi, this teacher of the art, enters
Reminds that wounds & imperfections
Can become our greatest strengths, as we embark on
Journeys of patient self-reflection and discovery.

Stories trumpet of resilience, decency and humanity
Born from treading treacherous terrains of malady,
We climb, steadfast, with unyielding steady pace,
Towards the light of wellness, like sunrise in rain.

Hope

In this creeping winter,
I dream white & pink cherry blossoms
slowly opening their drowsy eyes
to welcome warmer days.
It is in the freezing heart that I remember
the marvel of roses in their tender satin hues.

It is during these lashing wild winds
when the bamboo's brave resilience is tested,
it's bowing but not breaking comes to mind.
And I know that the emerald grass will win,
warrior-like — over dimming fields of snow.

Yes, I see winter as a friend, freezing,
maybe abandoned, but hopeful,
just waiting like you and me
for spring's miraculous rebirth.

Rough Edges

It has been a year of rough edges,
and so many tragic moments —
few pleasant surprises lurking.

Variants wickedly parading,
fascist signs and behavior —
maliciously marching in plain sight.

Truths — covered and uncovered
Unthinkables pouring in, almost normalizing.
The fate of climate in faltering hands.

Democratic principles shaky and under peril —
beware of being pushed around:
we are in what could be a tragic game...

What to do and how to win — unanswered questions
queuing for swift, yet feasible answers.

Tintinnabulation

A bell's toll echoes for reckoning, a call to healing.
A proclamation, statement, announcement of
something we cannot decipher: maybe a birth,
celebration, or death, a warning, even a threat,
a command, a call to order, an awaited change.

And it tolls for you and me — a signal for awakening:
"Be conscious, vigilant, be a visionary!"
Each of us interprets the ringing differently.
Still, it communicates — tintinnabulation —
with no words —

perchance for some — even close to divinity.

Life is Vibrant and Powerful

Nature too — with or without the pandemic.
That life force in us struggles and endures,
learns to work around obstacles like water,
finds its own distinct way to BE while moving.

How the bamboo copes with wind and rain,
adapting with innate flexibility, like our bodies do.
Does not resist so as not to break — bends, bows
with respect to warring winds without surrendering.

There is hope, yes, and doses of faith too,
the universality of our human condition.
Adapting to life's storms like pine and bamboo,
remaining present in the fullness of NOW.

To illumine pathways for others, as others,
like warriors of peace, have paved paths for us.

Inside These Monastic Days

I peek out from the inside
of these monastic days, venturing
to give life another chance again

in a created niche I name Contentment — amidst
an unpredictable pandemic, weighing life as is —
precious or empty, to learn to make peace,

flirt with seclusion's unique tranquility,
to simply be with me, measuring life as IS.
with lesser interventions from "out there,"

to fashion a life of quietude in the very midst
of mounting red lights of nosos and thanatos,
the "how of living," coping in a remoteness embrace

within a spatial niche — and breathe deep.
Bound to this cloistered life of stillness, loving,
learning what meditations mean without haste.

For there is little to hurry to, to hurry for,
a process of staying put: "to do nothing unnatural"
the 'wu wei' way— no reason to make haste —
my father's reminder: "festina lente."

A taste of life in chosen stillness,
having time to embrace this moment.
A permanence of brief moments
pile up like raindrops.

Inside, a soul bathed in light.
Outside, the world waiting for light.

Hope

Are we like a burning candle of old?
Is that not the truth?
Giver of light and beauty
throughout its short life — we think:
What is there to mourn when it's done?
We have the light within —
burns on, without burning us,
connecting to the Higher Light
that ignites yet another candle,
never doused — this glowing —

of what we may name Hope.

Time of Gardens

To keep my sanity, I have looked to the
lush green shades of trees, to the
rose, hibiscus, dahlia, & peony bush,
how their beauty seeps through
to the "inner garden" of the aching
heart & soul – maybe, just maybe,
transformations can blossom & grow
in the "wu wei" manner of the Daoist,
naturally — a transition like water or light
finding its way effortlessly from outer to inner realms
where no gateway blocks it to the Self,
where clarity may find its nook.
I take refuge in Rumi's celestial poetry
of love and devotion — words that delight,
bubbling from deep within the heart.

This life, this moment we have,
gifts us a new opening
to fill that emptied cup.

A Flight in Light or Darkness

Dawn shines with the virgin light of day —
a flight into past-present knowns: failures of many past
armed interventions that still haunt us, & unknowns of
  present ones glaring for solutions:
What will happen to the ocean of struggling humanity in
  Afghanistan?
The weight of what must be carried — dragged on,
then leave some behind as some tire of unsolvables.

Covid uncertainties, political dueling, few possibilities of
  achieving peace & democracy in so many countries.
We let go of most of it in the fast-approaching dusk of
  events,
hoping to take a final dip in the light of hopeful dawns.
To dream briefly, with what we've got left — visions of
  courage in the perfect imperfectness of it all.

Touched the good — those partially saved &
the not so good — those left in pain & despair.
Seeing through the vagueness — to try to comprehend,
living in what is — for that's all that remains.

A never-ending journey — as though through desolate
    mountains and valleys,
amid the tortuous climb whether in Covid-19 traps, or
    Afghanistan realities.

Still, in our heartfelt dreams,
living a sustained reality —
being in the i-n-g's,
there lies hoping, loving, caring to reach out.

Do only rules of the heart count?
But then, there are no rules there.

The Pandemic Span

The pandemic span of a seeming
forever emptiness taught me
without my intention —
to effortlessly scout
and dive into the stillness
within my Being.

An unintended contentment
of exploring — unwinding — dusting —
ironing out tangled internal threads of thoughts
piled up in my memory cave
from long neglected days.
There was time — plenty of it —

to ponder the moments, as if enlarged
in the milieux of an expansion of seclusion.
Call it a gift — though forced on me
by a vicious virus that killed.
I turned the bewildering lurking
into an exploration of thought digging.

A valued quest on the path of transformation.

Section 2 – The Dao of the Warrior

This section delves into the multi-dimensional essence of the warrior archetype, capturing its manifestations in the various walks of life. From the everyday heroes navigating life's complexities to the disciplined practitioners of the martial arts, this collection of poems honors the warrior in all its forms.

Here, the warrior is not confined to a single, rigid definition. Instead, it is a versatile and evolving archetype, embodying resilience, courage, and adaptability. Poems in this section celebrate the warrior spirit as it manifests in diverse scenarios.

In the midst of the global pandemic, the warrior spirit was evident in the resilience of both ordinary people and those in the medical profession.. They faced unprecedented challenges, yet continued to hope, adapt, act, heal, and triumph. Their struggles and victories offer a modern-day interpretation of what it means to be a peaceful warrior.

Another facet of the warrior spirit shines through individuals who refuse to remain silent in the face of political and social injustices like the brave women in Iran. These are people who fearlessly raise their voices, peacefully take to the streets, and use inclusive platforms to advocate for

change. Their courage to speak out and stand up for what they believe is right, adds a vital dimension to our understanding of what it means to be a warrior in today's world.

Another one of my aims has been to present the importance of the military treatise on war, namely "The Art of War" ascribed probably to Chinese strategist, Sun Tzu which formulates the strategic planning and conduct of war.

His analysis, written over 2000 years ago in China, specifies that the most important factor in war is the morality of government, especially of the leader who – if he governs justly, benevolently, and righteously, will follow the Right Path.

"Dao," has mutiple translations in different contexts, usually rendered as "The Way". Here, it is rendered as "moral influence", which SunTzu points out, maybe even more important than weaponry; although in battle, weather, terrain, command, and doctrine are also significant factors. It is fascinating to employ his 13 chapter treatise on the art of war to the war Russia has imposed on Ukraine which I have attempted to do in three of my poems. In the final analysis, Sun Tzu believed that the art of war is to win without fighting, and thus, ultimately, the art of peace.

In a world where conflicts still rage, the warrior spirit is poignantly exemplified by the Ukrainians' courageous defense of their country. Facing overwhelming odds, they have displayed an extraordinary blend of courage, resilience, and sacrifice.

Their struggle serves as a stark reminder that the path of the warrior is fraught with peril, whether chosen willingly or thrust upon them by destiny.

Lastly, the poems evoke the raw power and courage symbolized by majestic animals like the tiger. These creatures encapsulate the indomitable qualities that define the warrior spirit—strength, courage, and an unyielding will to overcome.

So, as you journey through this section, may you find reflections of your own warrior path, and may these poems inspire you to embrace the warrior within.

War Path

The Persian poet Saadi (8th century AD), wrote a poem that ornates the entrance to the United Nations building:

> *The children of Adam are limbs of one body,*
> *created of one essence.*
> *If destiny brings pain to one limb,*
> *the others cannot rest in peace.*
> *If you don't feel sorrow*
> *for the pain of others,*
> *you are unworthy of being called 'human.'*

Are tomorrows, empty promises in Ukraine?

Past invasion scars: Eastern Europe, Georgia, Crimea,
Chechnya, Syria. Spring hiding its daffodils, tulips, irises
   as missiles, bombs, & pain rain on Ukraine,
tanks roll on, rubble & blood cover the earth.

"We have to be faster than those who try to track us!"

Fear-frozen faces cry out, homeless hollers echo in empty
   streets.
Columns snake their way like forceps – east, north, south,
   west

56

All join invasion's ruins: battered ghost cities, collapsed
  buildings, wreckages wrapped in blood,
Dwindling supplies, trapped corridors, burning waste-
lands.

Nuclear alert? Hoodwinking the world? War crimes?

The helpless letter Z, prisoner of war, tortured into
  a symbol of aggression."Slava Ukraini" slogan of resis-
tance,
an insult hurled at Russia – once banned by Soviets,
  now a battle cry – swept into the halls of immortality.

Are bravery & blue yellow flags under siege too?

Italians sing for Ukrainian brothers and sisters:
bella ciao, bella ciao…. Who's listening? A world on edge.
Who's there? The Ukrainian peoples' epic battle.
Time strikes bullet fast, sanctions drain slowly.

Will the sunflowers & nightingales survive the onslaught?

When food, electricity & water disappear, fake stories
  from Russia appear

Stark realities stare: evacuation corridors shelled, cities
   flattened like pancake
some stay, some leave, Iron Curtain follows fleeing
   refugees.
Kamyshin & railways dodging attacks, repairing daily.

*Heroes of resistance forces? Those who know Ukraine will
win!*

Does hope or hunger die last? Where's the light?
The present extends – make or break moments.
A fork in the road: pick zero flexibility & more slaughter,
or a secret negotiation miracle to end escalation horrors.

How – that one person can hurt so many.…

Dialogue with Sun Tzu

*Across 25 centuries, I hear your words on the Art of War,
unambiguous like the radiant sun.*
War is the road to survival or ruin, life or death, so clear
calculations must be made.

What are the factors in this calculation?
Commanders who master these factors win, those who
don't, lose.
1st: moral authority of the ruler; 2nd: weather; 3rd:
terrain; 4th: command: a general's wisdom and
humanity;
5th: the army's organization & flexibility.

How do you know which side will win?
Which ruler possesses moral influence? Which
commander is more able?
Which army has the advantage of weather & terrain?
Which side better carries out regulations & instructions?

How do you conduct war?
Warfare is based on deception. So anger the enemy, con-
fuse him,

pretend inferiority, encourage his arrogance,
keep him under strain, & wear him down.

What is most significant in war, Master Sun?
Know yourself, and know your enemy. (zhi ji zhi bi)

What are other things to consider?
Attack the enemy's plans, worst is to destroy cities, best to
   take them intact.
Those skilled in war, cultivate the Dao, the way of human-
ity & justice.

You say moral authority is more powerful than weapons?
Yes, the art of war is ultimately to win without fighting,
   it is, in fact, the art of peace.

*Master Strategist of the art of war! Who will be the ultimate
   winner?*
The aggressor may think he has won by battling Ukraine,
   but he is bound to lose the peace.

The Rose that Knows

It's after Thanksgiving.
I walk up our street before
I turn into Calle Barcelona.

There's a house —
with American and Ukrainian flags
on the porch, waving in the wind.

A rose bush in front
with one red rose
that has stretched its neck

all the way up
to reach the flags.
Is this a family who made it out?

Their hearts red like the rose,
bleeding inside —
in this, their adopted land.

You Walk the Path Today

The Dao knows it well
no planning — just the *wu wei*.
It takes you where you must —
the natural spontaneous way.

It happens the way it should
with or without intent — flowing
like the river with no regrets
that knows to flow effortlessly,

moves along passing obstacles anyway.
Free and steady, without complaints,
the passage of life rolls on —
one stage to another.

You proceed, holding hands
with life's many hands
through chagrin, through bliss
and the enumerable in-betweens

like ordinary days
which are usually the best —
they keep the routine, the balance:
from highs of clapping and joys you see

like a hummer hovering on hibiscus,
to lows of apathy and dourness
like thinking "what a dull day!"
The savior is the bliss within,

the smile of tender feelings
gifting contentment:
"What a quiet healing day after all!"
To feel the joy out there —

like love of a grandson surprising you
with a bouquet of red roses,
or a friend's unexpected phone call.
It is all about when the bliss inside, meets the joy

on the outside — and
coincidental magic transpires,
and says:"This is your life!
Live it well!"

A Tiger Lives Fearless

In a single brief glance, the tiger spies its prize.
"Act like a man of thought, think
like a man of action!" says Thomas Mann.
Does the tiger instinctively do that?

It masters adaptations
to achieve its real wants –
in dense areas of vegetation –
spots its prey from its forceful snare.

Like a warrior, the tiger knows
action is the path to success!
Is destiny shaped through our actions
or avoidance of actions?

As a Chinese tale tells us, there were violent demons
on earth causing destruction and harm,
so the Jade Emperor called on the tiger
to defeat them. And he did.

So in 2022, Year of the Tiger, he was the guardian, embodying strength with courage and hope — and we shifted from pandemic to endemic, finally from discouragement and despair to hope.

The Open Window

We navigate the unknown —
free and open like a summer window view
to embrace the mysterious lurkings

to find what is deep in unsteady hearts
unlike joys of the past taken for granted
we take to flight – away from seeming

 inevitables that want to mire us
in the mist of present unknowns.
The only choice – to fly away from the gloom

searching in the dream mountain monasteries
for the enlightened in the midst of opposites —
to find the light they possess – one that opens

the secrets of *doing nothing*
unnatural — like Daoist seers —
while accomplishing much.

We yearn, we meditate —
to realize how and why
to dwell in tranquility.

Today, My Dear,
There's Little Time for Rest

No time for lingering — these uncertain times,
divide too wide to be re-stitched to fit.
No occasion to drowse when truth's dissembled
& few dare speak to call the fouls.

So do not go back to dreaming when donkey
& elephants — butting heads, hoof to crush.
No time to go back to heavy wishful sleep
when rule of any ONE replaces rule of law.

Time to awaken — not wallow in numbing fear
when guns turn arbiter & rattle louder than cash
there's no time left for slumber cached —
when it's becoming like the Wild Wild West.

How can you sleep a wink or go on a quest
when oceans & lands are tainted with trash
no time to idle in sweet slumber, my dear,
as abortion protections are rescinded away.

How may you sleep in a peace without panic
when line between church & state grows blurry,
when some hearts grip from fear to venture out
whether black, brown, slanted eyes or "hejabist,"

can you close your eyes to all of these?
How in good conscience can you roll in oblivion
when minds & bodies cry out for help?
When no seer nor sage dares show up to uplift.

Can you in good faith relax when hearts are tense
& even on Independence Day, they shoot to kill?
When the message in your brain chants:
"Cry, the beloved country!" you — only weep & weep,

for you cannot, in truth or stark reality – yield or flee.
Still, wise action tempered with audacity is what we need,
but how, how to close eyes to these – when "woke"
is somersaulted to please a few & race — colors views?

Can you lie low in all fairness to play blind & deaf?
When some, camouflage the truth for power & gain?
When hatred & prejudice armed armed with guns,
while masquerading with the blindfold of justice?

Time to waken & dislodge the consuming hate —
replace it with compassion & know how —
beyond the January 6th fray of strife & discord,
to replace — with listening to the other side.

A kind of "political kintsugi" we desperately need for
repair.

When the dark shell of hostility is broken, & truths
stare you in the face — maybe the message can be read.
"Build consensus, return to unity
where democracy is center."

Asked in 1787 whether the United States
has a monarchy
or a republic,
Ben Franklin ominously replied:

"A republic – if we can keep it!" Today we may cautiously
add: a republic & a democracy – if we can keep it.
What is really going on today? Are we truly
conscious of the fateful decisions we collectiverly make?

The Warrior Adapts

Tactics fluid, ever-changing,
high to low, a hawk's swoop,
then a sudden stall, hovering
before the strike.
Unpredictable.

Never one creature for long,
transforming,
water battering stone into submission,
fire caressing metal until it yields,
wood splintering earth.

In this theater of war,
amid steel meeting steel,
cries and shouts,
not just the man, but
the elemental warrior emerges.

The Marksman

Actions we take can be couched in hope, indifference,
passion, reluctance, or despair. To live fully, we pick Hope
as companion, welcomed like a boat during flood.

So much running that feels like standing still. Yet —
step by step, we break up unsolvables into pieces
to figure out — one "quark" at a time.

Though fragmented, possibilities peek, and rise like
rainbows over mountains we learn to climb — believing
we can make it to the summit — sometime.

Taking time to breathe in and out — the *chi* — to bond,
hold hands with this friend in exhaustion times,
repeating "Onward!" our marching mantra.

Leaving complacency behind, just the will to carry on,
even if ascents seem to have no ending for us. That tough
inner impulse, a clarity of focus and faith, as a light on the

hilltop that beckons like a marksman knowing the center.

Warrior Speaks of Victory

Observe the bamboo —
bends with the wind, yet never breaks.
Bend with the universe's way,
to resist snapping, a dry twig forgotten.

Consider the river —
it seeks not to overpower the boulder,
but flows around, persistent and patient,
till the boulder is pebble, carried in its embrace.

Note the flame —
burns not to consume, but to gift a light.
Your power within — not for destruction,
but a beacon to vanquish the dark foe beyond.

A battle won in blood
leaves earth scarred and hurt.
A war won on moral grounds — earth flourishes,
enemy not crushed, yet lifted by wise calculation.

To manifest in adversity, pathways to harmony
tear away from power's avarice and aggression
towards its strength to launch peace not subjugation,
displaying the kintsugi of compassion,

exemplifying true triumph in equanimity
reversing meanings of war
not necessarily, a zero sum game.
Where the ultimate picture

in reality — seems to be of two losers — just one more
the loser than the other! When cities and farmlands lay
broken and destroyed —where the benefit of ignoring
dead hearts or weary warriors,

for chimeras of glorious conquest are
like the mirage of desert water.
Victory, not just a fulfillment
of your aim...

but the cosmic design for harmony,
the silent command of the Unseen.

The Art of Peace

As Russia's invasion of Ukraine drags on — — —

We ponder more thoughts of war
Sun Tzu's "Art of War," — whispers a vision of insights.
A revelation borne from a timeless 25-centuries-old warrior,
Victory not only through battle, but through morality.

Consider, oh, weary warriors, before stepping onto the field,
Ponder, evaluate – is this bloody game worth the gambit?
Will you unsheathe your blade, engage in this dance with
    destiny?
A rehearsal of life and death, of victory or defeat,

Each move scrutinized, each breath a silent prayer,
Enter this arena, only when stakes match wisdom with resolve.
Sun Tzu speaks of the five pillars of warfare –
Five guiding lights piercing the somber fog that's war.

At the apex, stands moral influence, the Dao, the right path.
The unwavering compass of a sagacious leader,
Guiding earnest warriors, leading down a righteous path.
Behold, this terrain traversed, its hills and valleys,

The weather that holds sway over our lives,
The commanders that frame the force,
Humane orders cascading down the hierarchy,
Organizational order, sinew of any formidable force.

What fuels our march, what doctrine ignites the spirit?
All pertinent, all essentials in the theater – that's war.
Yet, he avers, above the clash of steel and roar of cannons,
Leader's moral backbone ultimately reigns supreme.

Cities besieged, destroyed – a sight Sun Tzu abhors,
The direst form of engagement, cowardice employed,
Best it is, he counsels, to capture cities intact,
To preserve humanity's soul of what once was.

Commanders on frontlines, they discern realities,
Grim battlefield truths, not a distant leader's fantasy.
In this grand charade of dark veils and threats,
Precision of intelligence, craft of deception hold sway.

If the enemy is at your doorstep, wear the guise of distant
    shadows,
When at hand, vanish into the specter of absence.
Deploy unseen eyes and ears, to gaze beyond the battlefield,
Decipher and disrupt the enemy's schemes.

Attack the enemy's stratagem, not his cities,
And grasp his tactics, untangling his web of battle.
Anger and confuse him, when united,
Divide him, wear him down.

Hence, the "Conduct of War".
Its heart beats for peace, a silent voice amidst the tumult,
Master Sun Tzu's legacy, a beacon through the ages:
"The Art of War is to win without fighting."

It is,
ultimately,
the art
of peace.

Unveiling the Scarf Rebellion

Was there a time in women's lives in some countries
when scarfs became a focal point of debate and dissent?

When formerly liberated women found themselves
trapped
in a revolution that snatched individual freedoms away?

Rules and regulations queued hard and strict: to wear
loose, drab-colored garbs resembling raincoats

to camouflage breasts and buttocks. At first the only
joy of rebellion came to be wearing colorful scarfs

on heads that were forced to conceal even a lock of hair.
Scarf shops multiplied and drawers filled with headscarfs

of all colors, sizes, and designs to cheer and comfort
saddened hearts of women who had lost freedoms.

A rallying cry became "Wear colorful scarves to rebel!"
And so it came to pass that bright head-coverings not only

enlivened the dull grey life of women – it gradually spread
when they dared to wear vivid hues in everyday wear

saving hearts from boredom and depression – with multi-
colors of blue, green, orange, yellow,

symbolizing a creeping but potent movement proclaim-
ing:"Women cannot be cowed

into submission!" Unusual "maghna'ehs" and headscarfs
became the fashion of the times

with loose long "lab coats" replaced by tight stylish outfits
and hair peeped out of scarves, followed by yet another

rebellion against strict "makeup rules"– one daring step at
a time to freedoms. Thus did an unpredictable rebellion

against a draconian dress code explode — when thousands
of women dared to ignore some government rules.

****

And then jarring — when a hardline president popped out
of the ballot box, with no compromise on hejab rules.

"Morality police" kills young Mahsa Amini in custody —
and a women's volcano erupts: school girls cut hair

79

in streets and town squares, others burn scarves in bonfires, and slogans of government defiance echo in the

dark of nights on balcony and roof tops. Thus did arrests and bloodsheds, mournings and pain ensue.

The scarf rebellion was on — and much more was in the country's destiny. Now — every woman could be Mahsa.

And so the streets ring with the contagious rallying cry of *"Zan, Zendegi, Azadi!"* Women! Life! Freedom!

***

*A year later, in 2023, the Scarf Rebellion of Iran's women
has succeeded in ways not dreamed of before -- but still has
a winding uphill journey ahead. And so today, a great ma-
jority of girls have won this battle by bringing about a sys-
tem-transforming change in many norms, in what seemed
unchangeable for over four decades* ago.

Acknowledgements

Grateful acknowledgements must go to the poets who conducted poetry workshops in Iowa and California where I was inspired and guided along the exciting path of poetry. My greatest gratitude and joy on this adventure goes to my son, Ali Arsanjani, who has been my faithful companion, my source of unfailing support and encouragement throughout these years. Without his wise counsel, comments and feedback, this book would never have been born to live. So many discussions, workshops, and debates we've had have enlightened me, triggering precious ideas and memories.

I have been influenced by enumerable master poets of the past, like Rumi and contemporary ones like Mary Oliver. My many years in Iowa gifted me many poet friends such as Lucille Morgan Wilson (former editor of Lyrical Iowa), Ron Kahl (former President of IPA), Dawn Terpstra (current President of the Iowa Poetry Association), Rod Reeves (First Vice President of IPA), Marilyn Baszczynski (editor of Lyrical Iowa), Bill Graeser, Pat Bieber and others. I was fortunate to have communicated with Lucille for years not only through workshops, but through the exchange of frequent emails. In addition, with the wonderful opportunity offered by the Society of Great River Poets, I was fortunate to participate in the weekly

Saturday poetry workshops held in Burlington and Mount Pleasant, organized by my dear friend Rod Reeves, and other Iowa poets.

Grateful acknowledgement and special thanks to my dear friend Rodney Charles, Editor and Publisher extraordinaire with his wit, humor and calm demeanor making the most difficult things possible.

In California, I am deeply indebted to my mentor and friend, Steve Kowit, who through his invaluable Sunday workshops in San Diego, and our email exchanges, gave me feedback and guided me on my poetic path for many years.

Special thanks to Michael Morse for taking the time to write the foreword for this book, and inspiring the notion of kintsugi in his poetry workshop during the pandemic.

In the words of Steve Kowit — who lives in the poetry I write everyday:

"... poetry is the music of the human heart and mind made manifest in language; at its most powerful and significant, it is the province not of a limited elitist coterie of "experts" and critics, but of a large, literate populace.

Poetry, in the end, is a spiritual endeavor. Though there is plenty of room to be playful and silly, there is much less room to be false, self-righteous, or small-minded. To write poetry is to perform an act of homage and celebration, even if one's poems are full of rage, lamentation, and despair. To write poetry of a high order demands that we excise from our lives as much as we can that is petty and meretricious and that we open our hearts to the sufferings of this world, imbuing our art with as luminous and compassionate a spirit as we can...."

—- from the introduction of Steve Kowit's *In the Palm of Your Hand.*

Afterword

*"Poetry is the spontaneous overflow of powerful feelings: it
takes its origin from emotion recollected in tranquility..."*
– William Wordsworth

This perspective of poetry is found in Wordsworth's
preface to his collection of poems titled "Lyrical Ballads,"
co-authored with Samuel Taylor Coleridge and published
in 1802, as an introduction to the collection and providing
insights into Wordsworth's poetic theory and philosophy.

In discussing the purpose and nature of poetry in that
preface, Wordsworth argues that poetry should be an ex-
pression of genuine emotions rather than a mere intellec-
tual exercise. According to him, poetry should arise from
powerful emotions that are experienced intensely and
spontaneously, emotions that can be triggered by encoun-
ters with nature, personal experiences, or even memories.

Wordsworth further explains that although poetry aris-
es from spontaneous feelings, it is shaped and refined
through the process of recollecting those emotions in a
state of tranquility. This means that after experiencing
intense emotions, the poet reflects upon them during mo-
ments of calmness and solitude.

It is during this reflective state that the poet gains a deeper understanding of
emotions, and can articulate them effectively through poetry.

These ideas of Wordsworth about poetry were revolutionary for their time. They challenged the prevailing poetic conventions, and laid the foundation for a new era of poetry. His emphasis on the expression of genuine feelings and the importance of personal experience, influenced subsequent generations of poets and had a lasting impact on the development of English literature.

* * *

As we come to the close of this collection, the evocative power of H.D.'s "Sea Rose" comes to mind. Many of the poems within these pages resonates with the spirit of the sea rose—a symbol of imperfection, resilience, and the transformative power of nature.

Much like the "harsh rose" that stands in stark contrast to the conventionally perceived rose, the verses here do not always speak of pristine moments or idealized feelings. They remind us that life's true essence is often found in the crevices of our imperfections. In the ebb and flow of life, we might find ourselves "caught in the drift" or "flung on the sand." Yet, it's not the act of being tossed by the tempests of fate but our response to them that defines us.

May God grant us the wisdom and strength. These poems celebrate this very resilience, echoing the sentiment that just as the sea rose is "more precious" due to its experiences, our lives, too, gain depth through trials.

Our existence, akin to the sea rose's dance with nature, is sculpted by myriad external influences. The poems in this collection, serve as testimonies to this sculpting, painting portraits of moments where external forces have acted upon the mind, soul and body. These forces sometimes gentle, often not — chisel our essence, making us who we are.

One of the profound messages carried by both the sea rose's acrid fragrance and the verses in this collection is the discovery of inner strength in adversity through the grace of God, our determination, support of friends and family, and sometimes just grit.

"Kintsugi," much like the Imagist principles that breathe life into H.D.'s poem, emphasizes authenticity. In a world increasingly veiled in pretense, there's a refreshing and healing power in raw, genuine expression. The poems you have journeyed through, are testimonies to this kind of authenticity—a clear, heartfelt reflection of experiences.

To have traveled through "Kintsugi" is to have walked the shores where sea roses bloom, understanding that life's true beauty isn't in the unblemished but in the scars and stories that shape us. As you have moved forward, may you find hope in healing, fortitude in scars, and beauty in imperfections, much like the golden veins of kintsugi pottery or the resilient spirit of the sea rose.

* * *

The poems in this collection have encompassed both worldly experiences, and also the dynamics and journeys that occur within the subtlest levels of consciousness, such as those encountered during moments of reflection, stillness and meditation.

Such poems have emanated from those ethereal moments, almost sacred junctures when the early morning stillness permeates, and consciousness has a momentary harmony with the universe's subtle melody.

In this state of serene receptivity, boundaries between inner and outer realms dissolve, beyond everyday thoughts, and grant access to more profound insights and heightened comprehension that may elude the mundane confines of everyday existence.

While many people may enjoy reading poetry for the imagery and concepts it evokes, I believe there is more to be discovered, like poems conveying the clear experiences of the mind and consciousness. These expressions may feel abstract to some, but are, in fact, empirical accounts of what transpires at those subtlest levels of the mind. Emotions and feelings arise whether from moments of tranquility, turmoil, or all the in betweens, sometimes blending our inner and outer worlds into a seamless whole. The voice within whispers – giving expression and meaning to what is observed in the external world.

I would like to share with you that my poems have also been influenced by two of the greatest of Persian mystical poets, namely, Rumi and Hafez. Persian poetry, with its soft, singing and melodic quality, has endowed the poetry with euphonic words – and these I hear, maybe even unconsciously, as I write my lines. The heritage is there – as I remember Mom and Dad reciting from memory, famous lines from their favorite poets – even as I express my thoughts in English poetry. It is a quest, a journey of the heart that embraces a life of the seeker.

I believe a poem achieves its multifaceted goals when the narration comes alive — you are there vicariously with the poet, seeing, feeling what the poet is describing. A poem succeeds if the reader remembers the poem, leaving an indelible impression on the mind. If you are sitting in the movie theater watching a movie, then reading a poem is like splashing unto the screen and almost becoming part of the tale!

I see poetry as a form of painting in organized or intuitive thoughts expressed in words that speak to you directly or mysteriously, that flow from mind and heart as though dancing on the page, injecting thoughts of wonder and curiosity. With its imagery, it relates a story that makes you ponder or visualize the world from perspectives you never conceived — feelings that may reverberate or communicate the joys and tribulations of life.

A good poem moves you, inspires you, and may take you to another world. It can be like a seed planted in the mind — what flower will it create? What idea will it sprout into your world that will move you forward on thought-paths you never trekked before? Poetry is an adventure you pursue to unlock unknowns — whether in a major or minor key — to thoughts and worlds uncharted. It takes you on journeys untravelled. Words have the power to deeply impact, even transform us, whether by touching our hearts, enlightening our minds, or changing perspectives on life, even inspiring us to take action. A poem's magic is there if it describes the 'feel' of time and place: a feeling — that you are there! And you want to read on!

Maryam Daftari
Carlsbad, California
August 2023

Printed in the USA
CPSIA information can be obtained
at www.ICGtesting.com
CBHW040055170924
14584CB00020B/55